A venture through broken thoughts

ANANNYA SWAMY

BookLeaf Publishing

India | USA | UK

Presentation by *BookLeaf Publishing*

Web: www.bookleafpub.com

E-mail: info@bookleafpub.com

ISBN: 9789363315723

First edition 2024

*To my parents and family, whose unwavering
love and support have been my guiding light.*

*To my friends, who have shared in my joys and
sorrows and who have inspired me with their
own stories.*

*And to the readers, who breathe life into these
words and give them meaning.*

Thank you for being a part of this journey.

ACKNOWLEDGEMENT

This collection of poems would not have been possible without the support, encouragement and inspiration from many wonderful individuals.

First and foremost, I would like to thank my parents, whose unwavering support and love have been my greatest source of strength. Your belief in me has made this journey possible.

A special thanks to my friends and fellow writers who have inspired me with their own creative journeys and provided critical feedback on my work.

I am also grateful to my roots in Kerala and my life in Madhya Pradesh, Nagda, for enriching my experiences and influencing my writing.

Lastly, to every reader who finds solace, joy or reflection in these poems, thank you for taking the time to delve into my world. Your presence gives life to my words.

With gratitude,
Anannya Swamy

PREFACE

Poems are a collection of states that are hard to define in definite words. As a poet, I sought to incorporate every aspect of emotional turmoil within these pages. Each poem represents something distinct yet interconnected, offering a unique glimpse into the various facets of the human experience. They connect and differentiate from one another in equal measure.

Allow these poems to sink in as you read, embracing the journey through each emotional landscape for a richer and more profound experience.

Illusion Of Us

There was a perfect dream, crafted by me for us,
Which was fragile like glass.
Everything that was ever done seems to be in
vain,
As the question 'why' creeps up:
Why does it end up like this? Did everything
that was done mean anything?
Promises made along the path seemed futile,
Shattered or broken into pieces that can't be
repaired.

Dreams that carried us through dimensions of
my delusion,
Creating a bond unbreakable for me,

But alas, you and I were never meant for each
other.
You proved that by uttering those pathetic
words,
'You deserve better'.
But why better when I want you? When I trust
you? When the only thing I wished for was your
happiness?

Oh yeah, the happiness that I wished for you.
Does that mean your happiness lies beyond us?
I guess my wishes have come true, but accepting
it is unbearable.
You chose wisely for yourself,
Making me feel like a loving fool.
Thank you for proving
That when you give your heart to someone,
It's often returned broken.

A Midnight Thought

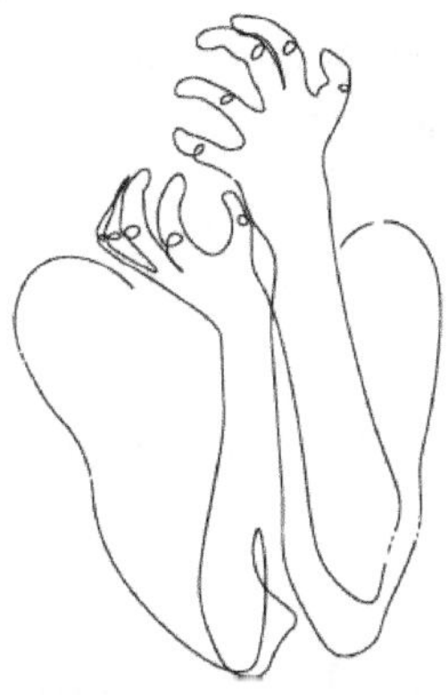

A midnight thought of a broken heart,
With it's grieving in silence, that's unknown to
the world,
That wrenches the heart, and the soul crumbles
with sadness,
As a million pieces of glass bleed the heart,
stings of pain rise from every piece, which feels
less than the pain suffered with a broken heart,
Promises made in past feel as a heavy burden to
the soul,
Each tearing something apart within, with same
intensity,
An unknown cry emerges with sorrows of the
past,

Sorrows, which were hidden in some dungeon of
the heart,
Heavy feeling settles through the soul,
A midnight thought that fills me with grief of a
never-ending sadness

Sometimes It's Just Me And My Thoughts

Sometimes it's just me and my thoughts,
Coaxing me to be alone, to be lonely,
Making me feel as a burden in everyone's eyes,
Staying in the cage of my room feels appealing,
Loneliness just seems another reason for not
interacting with people,
Sometimes it's just me and my thoughts.

Thoughts being so intrusive that make my mind
go numb,
Thoughts make me distance myself just for my
own self-assurance,
The feeling of being inadequate fills me up,
Sometimes it's just me and my thoughts.

The room, which should make me feel safe,
feels suffocating,
Giving me evidence of my incompatibility,
Laughing at me for they're being empty,
Reminding me of the people I caused hurt to,
Scratching my scars deep down, making me feel
useless,
Sometimes it's just me and my thoughts.

Desires

I have a desire to give in to my desires,
To let the whispers of misery take over me,
To let my self-confidence wither away,
To let my overthinking prove its rights,
To make myself miserable in front of everyone,
To laugh at my own insecurities,
To make fun of myself,
To let myself fall into the dilemma of my own
delusions,
To conspire against myself.

Desires that drive me crazy,
Imagining myself at my weakest points,
Stretching their arms towards me, pulling me
backwards,
Trying to break my will to stand firm.

Desires that come and go like waves,
Proving their uncertainty,
Making me hope for myself a little,
To let myself create a barrier against my own
desires,
I grip onto my strength, standing up for myself,
When I no longer believe in myself,
I have a desire to give in to my desires.

Frantic Heart

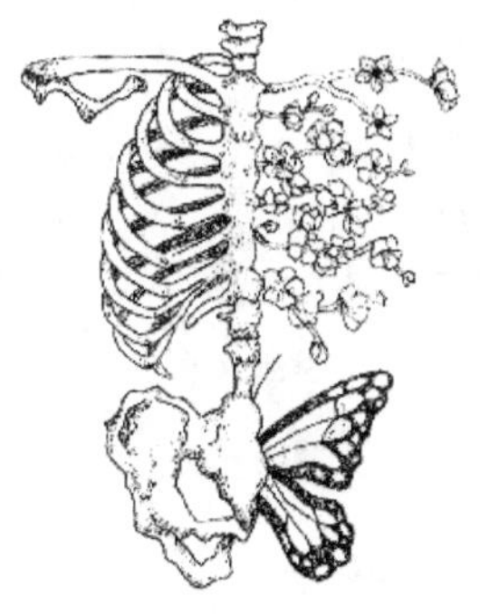

Heart thumping against
hollow, rigid bones,
trying to make sense,
yearning to leave.

Emptiness moulds itself
like a swarm of bees,
buzzing, restless,
within the walls
of my ribcage.

Handling sufferings,
trapped in seeds of hope,
heart crying out,
a scream in the void,
caught in a frantic haze.

Clutching To Yesterday

I caged all moments,
Happy or sad, in a corner of my heart,
Securing them with all my might.

People hovering around,
Saying to let them fly,
Free them from the cage,
In assurance of my own freedom.

Covering my ears, I disregard them,
Their disappointed faces meet my eyes,
My eyes that portray my pathetic love,
My last effort to savour it in myself.

The desperation of saving the moments,
That made me laugh and cry,
Filled me with joy that seemed never-ending.
I find myself wondering,
Can my desperation give me the moments back?

Scars Of Time

They say that time will heal me, yet my scars
remain,
A silent echo of my hidden pain.
When I break down, the wound feels fresh
again,
The past comes back, like shadows in the rain.

These scars remind me, they linger near,
Haunting my trust, feeding my fear.
The pain I thought was gone returns each day,
And I wonder, 'Am I healed, or just on display'?

Time may soothe me, but the memories stay,
Their haunting whispers won't go away.
Each new day forces me to act,
To wear this smile, to hide the cracks.

In this loop of pretending to be fine,
I bury my wounds; I draw the line.
They say time heals, but the memories remain,
And I'm left acting – just to endure the pain.

Whispers Of Silence

'Silence holds the secrets the heart dares not
utter,
Kept hidden in the corners, out of reach for
everyone.
Silence haunts you with those secrets,
As you pray for it to stop,
Silence mocks your gullibility,
Threatening self-destruction for its own
enjoyment.
It makes you regret your actions,
Silence taunting you for all of it,
Until you decide to break the seal,
Unravel the truth,
Brave in front of everyone.
Silence watches as you dance through it,
Growing braver to fight for yourself.
Silence no longer suffocates,
It comes with a calm that makes you sleep'.

Haunting Nights

Memories haunt in the silence of the night,
Night that reflects all the good and the bad,
Engulfing you within for the memories to knock
at your door,
Rushing inside your mind, reminding you of all
the memories like bubbles in a fizzy drink,
One by one, bursting with all the emotions that
send chills down your soul,
You feel emptiness inside your body as if your
organs and bones are all gone,
Left behind is just a hole,
As the night becomes longer, you struggle with
your memories,
Sleep that seems lost captures you within,
Silencing all your thoughts and memories,

In despair, you close your eyes as the night tries
to haunt you again with your memories.

Past Pain

Heart screams with the pain of the past,
The scars once more feel fresh.
For the world, I tried to be brave with a smiling
face,
But tears escape through my eyes unknowingly,
betraying me.
Bitter tears show the sorrows that were locked
up in the chambers of my heart,
Screaming, shouting, struggling to be let out
again for the world to see my weakness.
Wiping away the bitter tears, I stand facing the
world,
For I will never be weak again in front of
anyone.

My scars deep down remind me of my naivety in
the past,
For believing in people with all my heart.
But now, as I see myself tearing apart,
I promise myself to never back down, to stand
up for myself and to protect myself.

Soulful Surrender

Letting go of someone,
Is not just about them or yourself,
But breaking yourself,
Moulding yourself again and again,
Reshuffling your mind, body and soul,
Testing your patience,
Being alone when you crave them the most,
Carrying your broken trust,
Sadness that engulfs you,
Breaking your body into pieces,
Mind being aware of the emptiness,
Soul drowning in the pool of sorrow,
As misery takes over you.

Until you become brave again,
Your trust becomes rare to gain,

Making yourself unreachable,
Experiencing the confidence,
As you make emptiness your home,
Crafting your mind to be strong,
Synchronising your soul for the future,
Letting your ambition rise high,
Instilling trust in yourself,
Letting go of someone is not just a process,
But reviving and creating oneself.

Self-Worth

In the depths of uncertainty, you find yourself questioning,
It becomes a habit to doubt yourself without knowing your worth.
Are these doubts valid? Am I capable? Can I do it?
The questions swirl around your mind like bees around their hives,
Confusing you, eroding your self-confidence,
Questions that seem trivial but gain importance through overthinking.

Darling, you are the only person who can love
yourself unconditionally,
Allow yourself to breathe a sigh of relief,
Questions will be answered through your hard
work in due time,
Love yourself for trying, for improving, for
never giving up,
Love yourself even when you fail,
Because a little failure can't make you love
yourself any less.

Freefall Of Thoughts

Thoughts urging to escape,
Making moves to spill.
To shake society with unbridled speeches,
Thoughts of self-acceptance.
Asserting 'you hold no right to comment',
Being unashamed of the opinions thrown upon,
Embracing oneself, indifferent to others'
perceptions.

Lost In Contrasts

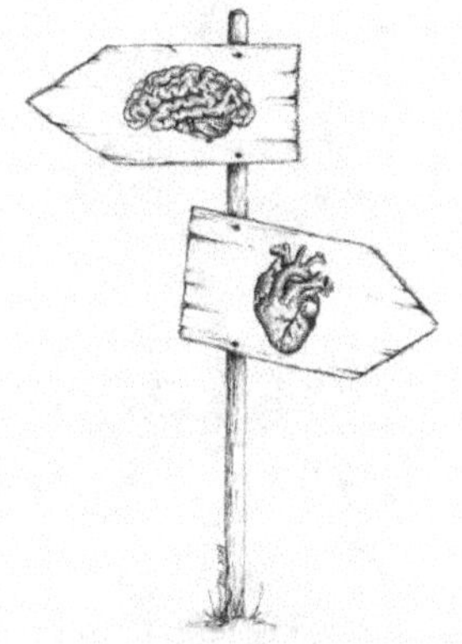

Lost between the desire for someone's
companionship but also craving the solitude to
be alone,
a companion to explore everything but also
solitude to find myself,
a person to hold hands with but also buying
chances to be alone with myself,
to be cared for but also to be seen by none,
someone being there in every situation but also
to hide tears in darkness,
lost between being heard, seen and listened to
but also wanting to be in loneliness, finding it
safe.

Secrets Of A Troubled Mind

Anxiety weaves through the cracks in my mind,
A restless echo I cannot leave behind,
Thumping inside my heart,
Restlessness evident in my hands,
Calming my mind with all sorts of phrases,
But anxiety wins the battle,
My mind growing numb as doubt becomes fear,
My heart collapsing against my ribcage,
Running away from the waves of fear,
Crying mercy as anxiety gains control,
It makes secrets known.

Puppets Of Uncertainty

Shared grief of
Unknown wars
Tears mixed with
Blood
Of souls sacrificed
With burdened choices
No one knows the
Roles to play
Just puppets in the
Hands of uncertainty

Unravelling Sanity

I see myself,
With blank eyes,
Emotionless face,
Soul filled with doubts,
Every inch of the body on the verge of insanity,

I see myself,
Destroying everything built with care,
Blankness of emotion taking over my mind,
Causing it to zone out and destroy itself,
Destruction evident in front,

I see myself,
Sinking into a deep abyss,
Consciousness no longer needed,
Abandoning my soul,
I let go of everything, including myself,
Killing everything within,
As the urge succeeded.

Innocent Heart

I find myself alone, wandering through thoughts,
While people around me seem to be enjoying,
In the busyness of the surroundings, a feeling of
being left alone creeps,
A feeling that cages my heart with fear,
Fear of being left behind, losing myself in a
world of unknowns,
In a world where every action is judged and
measured with its own tools,
My heart, with its innocence, tries to be strong,
giving me hopes of reassurance,
All I can do is laugh at my own heart's naivety
of the world,
Which is waiting for me to face it down,

But for once, I know that my weakness is only
for me to make fun of,
For the world, I am stronger than ever with all
the self-confidence bestowed within me.

Silent Courage

Oh, to the wonder that we're done thinking about
the endings that were never meant to be,
Oh, to all the things that were happy and sad for
which I wait,
Trying to be strong, letting go of that with a big
smile,
That has my emotions like something fragile,
breakable but not penetrable,
I tried to be mindful of everything and anything,
Trying and trying to be brave as the world sees
of me.

Agony's Whisper

Sounds of agony echo,
As emptiness surrounds me,
I hear the laughter of people,
Numbness covers my body like a blanket,
In the hours of busyness,
I find myself zoning out,
Feeling nothing other than agony,
Loneliness calls me for its embrace,
I surrender myself to it,
It consumes me like a desert,
I try to be indifferent to my surroundings,
As I no longer try to be appealing,
Just surviving my days,
With loneliness keeping me company.

Relief In Flames

Lighting up flames
To turn into ashes
Seeing myself burn
Letting it consume me
For love to be fair
Trying to remember pain
Flames pure with no bias
Giving me relief
Relief from loving
Betrayal, longing, all seems
To merge
Melting down in flames of
Self-destruction

Unchained Demons

A storm covered the sky,
Rage caged inside,
Destructing mindfulness,
Destroying the sanity left inside,
The rage grew intense,
Violating everything around,
Mercy lost in sorrow,
Eyes burning with revenge, unsettling emotions
swirl,
As destruction seemed evident,
Demons bred with care,
Consuming everything within.

Mourning Words

Tangled with unspoken
words,
heart drowning with the weight,
mind spiralling around to be
free,
demanding for reasons to be
quiet,
heart mourning for the loss of reason,
knowing words spoken would mean nothing

Haunting Heaviness

Heaviness settles in,
Clutching the body tight,
Invading privacy with authority,
Painfully sticking in,
Trying to be helpful,
Playing all the sins in one go,
Numbing the mind to internal sleep,
Sleep that makes tears burn,
Overthinking peaking its range,
Making it hard to clarify reality,
Illusion mixes with delusion,
As heaviness sinks in.

Deceptive Kindness

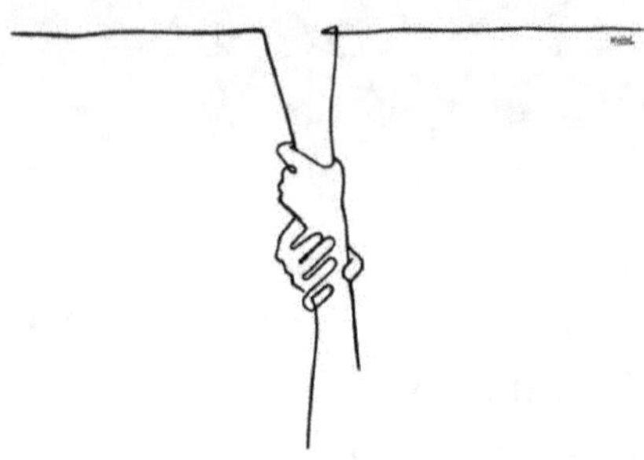

It says it will protect me,
From what I wouldn't know,
Creating barriers around me,
For it just needed to cage me,
In the pretence of protection,
Abandoning me there alone,
For me to helplessly call for it,
Realising words spoken with a kind face,
Are not always truths to be trusted.

Reviving Hope

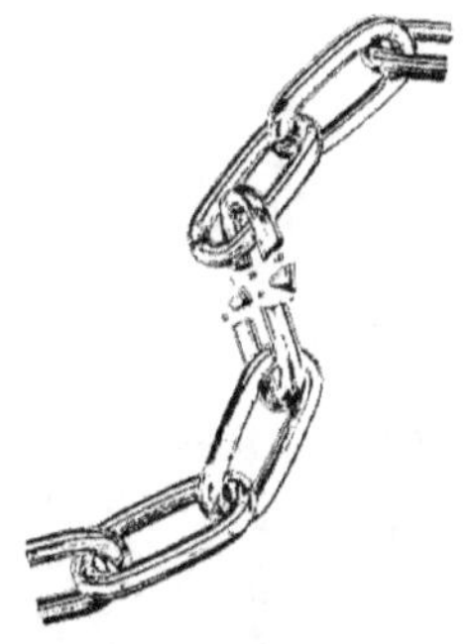

Tangled in my own delusions, I forget myself,
Trying to be like others, forgetting my real self.
Lowering myself in my own eyes,
I doubt myself, asking questions that let me
down.
I bind myself with chains of expectations,
Turning myself into misery,
The chains burden me to the point of
suffocation.
I try to regain consciousness, breaking
delusions,
Only to be thrown back.
I try again and again, delusions cracking,
I see hope for myself to regain and revive.
I hold on to it, making myself aware of its
beauty,
And soon, I break the chains of expectations.

Ants Of Despair

Peace is slowly being eaten,
Is it peace or loneliness? I can't tell the
difference.
Crawling on my body like ants, biting as if it's a
feast,
Consuming me entirely, too afraid to speak.
I watch as pain turns into numbness,
As it crawls and consumes every inch.

Imagination's Play

Twisted imaginations,
Gambling with the mind,
Taunting its incapabilities,
Laughing at its naivety,
For the mind just wants to play,
Never knowing the truth,
Of vague imaginations,
That will never stay.

Storm Of Doubt

Storm grows inside me,
Lighting striking my soul,
Every time I try to be confident,
Paving the way for self-doubts,
Breaking everything that was built,
Leaving pieces that seem hard to rebuild.

Cracks Of Vulnerability

I hear the sounds of cracks,
As I shatter in front of myself,
Crumbling into pieces of nothingness.

Piece by piece, everything falls and crumbles
before me,
I lie there, questioning myself for all my deeds.

My beliefs, my confidence, my naivety – all
shattering before me,
Their sound giving me clues to my ignorance of
myself.

Thinking about the things I've done wrong,
I blame myself for my incapabilities.

As I question myself, why does it have to be like this?
Am I so vulnerable to the world that I crumble every time?

But this time, as I shatter and crumble, I promise myself not to hope anymore.

Intoxication By Hatred

Hatred suffocates kindness,
Intoxicating veins.
Being betrayed each time
Now seems destined.
Trying to comprehend the inevitable,
Standing alone,
Feelings of worthlessness capturing my mind.
It's fatal to be kind
As it dies slowly every time.

A Growing Void

Beneath the warming sun, as I lie alone, away
from everyone,
Taking in the warmth the sun gives,
There is a chill that runs through my soul,
Reminding me of my loneliness,
Reminding me that even if the sun gives me
warmth, there is still a hole inside me that can't
be filled,
A hole that keeps growing with every second,
The emptiness inside it keeps telling me of my
incompetence,
It consumes me in my own delusions, even
though there is still the warmth of the sun.

Haziness Of Life

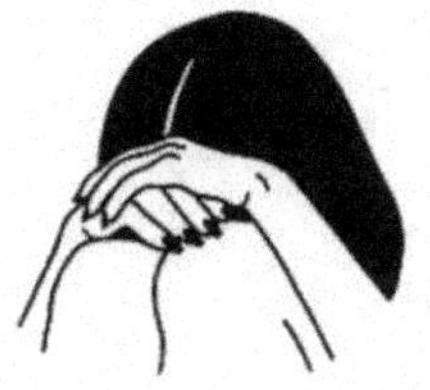

Scared to be broken again,
Fate has a fatal stand,
Trying to be brave for oneself,
Ended up destroying final hopes,
Which were lost in the depths of the haziness of
life,
Trying to grow but trapped in indecisiveness,
Chained with insecurities,
Which try to be fair in their judgment,
Making each next step questionable in life,
Stuck in loops of hopelessness,
When all that was needed was someone's trust,
Which never found its way.

Navigating Doubt

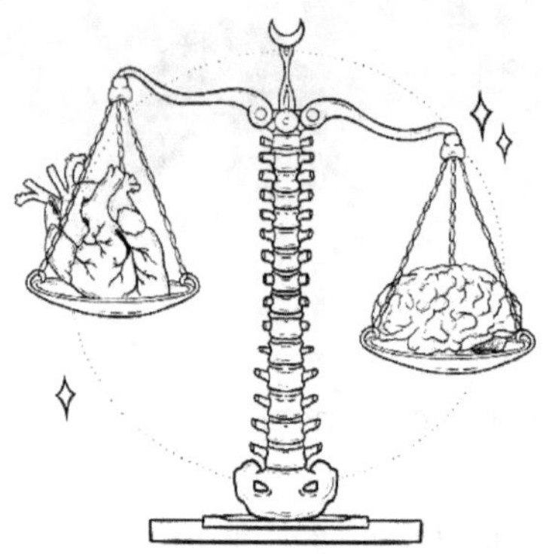

Scribbling through thoughts,
That engulf mindfulness,
Trying to escape their clutches,
Aligning thoughts for plans,
Calls of doubt submerge,
Becoming evident with each passing second,
Trying to be resourceful,
Making way for clear thinking,
Helping to smooth the mind's unevenness,
Dealing with doubts that
Haunt the mind.

Burdened By Inadequacy

Burdened with thoughts,
Broken by self-pity,
My soul restless within my own body,
Suffocated by expectations,
Overwhelmed by feelings of inadequacy,
Incapable of being helpful,
Burning my soul into ashes,
Which scream for their own grieving.

Reality's Invasion

I created a world for myself,
With all hopes and my illusions.
With care, I nurtured it,
Growing it alongside myself,
Protecting it from harsh realities
That try to break in,
Ignoring them to the fullest.
I live in a world of my own delusions,
But soon it crumbles,
As reality makes its way in.
My trust is broken, and protection no longer
safeguards my world.
Reality hits hard, making it impossible to ignore.
As my world crumbles before me,
I stand there, distorted, for the truth of reality is
cruel but true.

Blaming it becomes hard,
As I understand my naivety for being ignorant.

49

Isolation's Embrace

My soul feels heavy with each step,
As numbness soaks into it.
Heaviness keeps increasing,
As the ache that was lost comes knocking.

A similar sorrow engulfs me,
My mind robbed by pain,
Piercing through me.
Tears roll down my cheeks, leaving salted
marks.

Is it all worth it?
The scars buried inside remind me
Of foolishness that once seemed never-ending.

Giving another chance feels like mocking
myself.

How can I think about it?
Can I put myself through the suffering again?
The agony of being left alone
Gives scars that simple talk won't repair.

Trusting again feels burdensome.
Am I forever going to be like this?
Can I trust anyone again?
I embrace the loneliness given by those I trusted
most.

In a world full of people,
When I find myself lonely,
I accept it as my fate.

Shattered To Strong

Past suffering etched deep lines in my soul,
shaping who I am today,
Scars, wounds, betrayals reside deep inside,
Acting as lessons for the future,
Reminders of uncertainty,
For trusting people with all your heart,

Consequences of actions done unknowingly,
Buries deep inside, caging yourself from others,
Making you feel vulnerable in front of yourself,
Suffocating yourself through overthinking,
Delusion playing its role wisely,
Trapping you in chains of suffering,
Preventing you from stepping up once again.

You try and try with all your might,
Your soul praising you for your efforts,
Which seem futile, as hopes are crushed away,
Believing in yourself, breaking the chains,
Opening your heart a little to the world,
Letting yourself experience the hardships,
For it will pay back in the future one day.

A Heart's Hopes

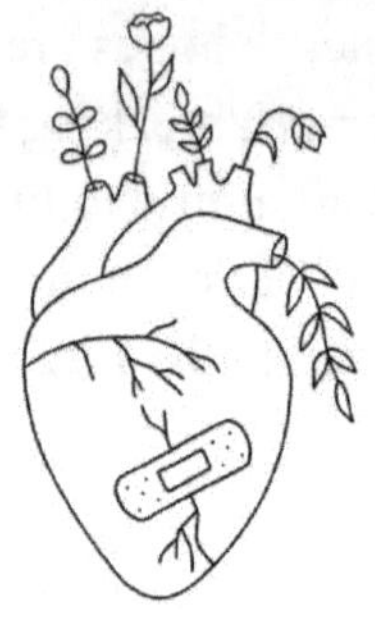

A heart with hopes,
Hopes of new beginnings,
Of better endings,
Hopes, which usually get crushed,
Hopes that keep you awake,
Hopes that inspires you to live,
Hopes that brings something new to keep going,
Hopes that each time destroyed, gets
reincarnated,
Hopes – that's all it takes to survive this world.

Oh, To Fall In Love With Myself

Oh, to fall in love with myself,
To leave behind the weight of opinions on the
shelf.
To stand by me, through thick and thin,
Supporting my heart, where love begins.

To throw tantrums, knowing they'll be met,
With understanding and no regret.
To let self-doubt simply pass by,
Without questioning my worth, without asking
why.

To be myself, through judgement's storm,
Unafraid, unyielding, in my truest form.
Oh, to be me – blissfully and free,
Eternally at peace with all I see.

Oh, to fall in love with who I am,
No more pretences, no need to cram.
To live in this love, forever divine,
For in this heart, I am always mine.